Disaster Survival Series: Book One

HURRICANE
PREPARATION & SURVIVAL

*Step-by-Step Lists
To Minimize Body and
Property Damage*

MEGY DAVIS

Copyright © 2019 by Megy Davis

All rights reserved. No part of this publication may be reproduced, distributed or transmitted in any form or by any means, including photocopying, recording, or other electronic or mechanical methods, without the prior written permission of the publisher, except in the case of brief quotations embodied in critical reviews and certain other noncommercial uses permitted by copyright law. For permission requests, please email the publisher with "Attention: Permissions Coordinator" in the subject line.

megydavis@megydavis.com

Ordering Information:

Quantity sales: Special discounts are available on quantity purchases by corporations, associations, and others. For details, contact the "Special Sales Department" at the address above.
Hurricane Preparation and Survival by Megy Davis- 1st ed.

ISBN-13: 978-1-7331417-0-3

Cover Photo by Maria Michelle at Pixabay

BONUS DOWNLOAD:
Request your printable PDF of the five checklists that correspond to this book by emailing:
megydavis@megydavis.com

TABLE OF CONTENTS

Introduction 1
Chapter 1   My Story 3
Chapter 2   What Makes a Storm a Hurricane? 6
Chapter 3   June First; Twelve Essential Actions 13
Chapter 4   A Ten Day Timeline for an Approaching Storm 19
Chapter 5   Riding Out The Storm 28
Chapter 6   Survival in Crisis Mode 38
Chapter 7   Three Types of Insurance 41
Chapter 8   Rebuilding Damaged Homes 45
Chapter 9   Useful Apps from your App Store 49
Glossary & Acronyms 51
Appendix 1   Storm Cupboard' Supply List 55
Appendix 2   Emergency Car Kit 57
Appendix 3   Hurricane Plan Outline 59
Appendix 4   Shelter Supply List 62
Appendix 5   Pet Emergency Supply List 63
Prayer 65
Author Biography 67

Taken by Aline Patterson

INTRODUCTION

If you have recently moved to a hurricane vulnerable area or are among the large percentage of property owners or residents living in a coastal area, you could lie in the path of a potentially life-threatening hurricane. This book is a must-read for you because hurricanes are serious business. Proper preparation can save your life, the lives of your loved ones, and your pet. The planet is currently in a weather pattern that annually packs a real punch to our coastline and inland areas. If your stomach tightens a little on June first each year, and you breathe a sigh of relief on November thirtieth (hopefully without a hurricane strike), then this ninety-minute read, and resource has been written for you.

Information and preparation are crucial to surviving these extreme tropical weather onslaughts. Loads of information is posted on countless internet websites detailing how to get ready for a tropical storm or oncoming hurricane. While researching this book, I combed through tens of thousands of excellent web pages. It was exhausting and time-consuming. It was also nothing I would care to be doing as a hurricane was churning its way toward me.

This book drills down the most relevant information I found into bullet points and lists. Included is a checklist of twelve 'must-do' actions to complete by June first when Hurricane Season begins. This checklist also outlines in detail proactive steps, conversations decisions you need to begin making. It also includes a checklist for pre-stocking your storm supply cupboard. These step-by-step preparations are for you to refer to, and use on an as-needed, ongoing basis as a hurricane approaches your coast.

As tropical storms progress toward your location, the next four lists *(Emergency Car Kit, Hurricane Plan Outline, Shelter Supply List and Emergency Pet Supply List)* may or may not come into play. At the very least, you have them to mark off as you complete them. Yes, take your pen out and write in this book or take e-book notes on your device. I have also included a section about your three most significant insurance policies, your insurance adjuster, Water Mitigation Services, Public Adjusters, and the best hurricane apps to download ahead of a storm.

Detailed information about hurricane storm systems, explanations for the lists and first-hand accounts by hurricane survivors are the framework of this book. A Glossary and Index of Acronyms are in the back of the book to help you decipher what the newscasters are referring to in their broadcasts. A prayer is included at the end because I have found most people cry out to God during these extreme circumstances. If you don't know what to say to Him, this prayer will benefit you, and help you begin a dialogue.

> Ben Franklin said,
> "By failing to prepare,
> we are preparing to fail."

I am a survivor of several hurricanes that have hit the east coast of Florida. I am also a Catastrophic Insurance Adjuster and have seen too much preventable damage and destruction from these storms in the past sixteen years. With the writing of this book, it is my sincere hope and deep desire to help YOU prepare for the high winds, substantial amounts of rainwater, and storm surge that can arrive with a Hurricane. I intend to keep you in the best position possible to minimize the potential heartbreak and damage a hurricane can cause.

> "The only two good things that can be said for a hurricane are that it gives sufficient warning of its approach and that it blows from one point of the compass at a time."
> Gertrude Atherton

1
MY STORY

AS A NEWLY single mom with two teenage boys and a dog, I was headed back to college and working three jobs. My primary source of income was as a professional wedding and school photographer in the Fort Lauderdale, Florida area. Life was going well in the fall of 2004.

Bam! Hurricanes Frances and Jeanne blew through South Florida causing havoc and chaos. Floridians had been spoiled and had not felt the strong winds of destruction since 1992 when Hurricane Andrew came ashore in a direct hit to metropolitan Miami. Luckily, my house was not damaged.

Unfortunately for me, couples canceled their wedding photos, and nobody cared about school pictures that year. Folks had more immediate concerns; no electricity or hot water and significant repairs to their homes and roofs. That Sunday at church I cried my financial blues to my friend Barry. He advised me to get my insurance adjusters license. Thus, if the same situation ever happened again, my source of income would instantly come from being a catastrophic insurance adjuster. That sounded good to me. Barry pointed me to a forty-hour course at the local college I was attending, and in June of 2005, I became a Florida licensed insurance adjuster.

I immediately went online and found a third party adjusting company who was giving free classes on the nuts and bolts of catastrophic adjusting. If you passed the course and they liked you, there was a job for you, should another hurricane approach. Approach they did; relentlessly! 2005 was the year of those three bad girls, Katrina, Rita and Wilma. I've heard them called worse.

Hurricane Katrina was a wet one and grazed the south part of Dade County, Florida on its westward journey. Katrina then ramped up as she crossed the Gulf of Mexico, to devastate New Orleans, Lousiana. I was busier than a termite in a sawmill, writing insurance claims seven days a week, eighteen hours a day. I remember desperately wanting to help as many insureds as I could, to recover from the Miami part of Katrina. I recall going into people's damaged homes, and their eyes would be transfixed on the TV screen — horrifying images of the desperate and stranded people in New Orleans. I barely glanced since I had to keep moving on to the next claim. We adjusters were working fifteen hours a day, seven days a week.

Things got quiet for about a minute. Then Hurricane Rita blew across the Florida Keyes. I wrote insurance claims down in Key Largo, and by mid-October, I was sick of looking at damaged refrigerators, washing machines, dryers, and toilets piled up along US#1, the only road in or out of the Keys. I didn't want to listen to one more sad, sad story of how peoples lives had been totally upended. It was the same story, always, and it seemed I'd heard it a million times.

Life finally quieted down again. Halloween decorations began to appear outside a few houses. It looked like I could finally take a day or two off and get the muffler fixed on my 1990 Eldorado. It had separated at the manifold and was embarrassingly LOUD. I always prayed the insureds would **not** be so kind as to carry my ladder back out to my car. I didn't want them to hear the ear-splitting, backfiring noise when I fired Old Eldo up. When they did, I made the weak joke that I was the Uncle Buck of insurance adjusters. Heh-heh.

Like spit-balls in a fifth-grade classroom, the swirling, white tropical storms on the television screens kept coming across the Atlantic the fall of that year. Floridians were hurricane-weary. One last one, Hurricane Wilma was supposed to turn north as it approached the Bahama Islands and not be a threat to South Florida. In the dark, early morning hours of October 24th, Wilma hit Grand Bahama like a spinning top at 95 miles per hour. The force of the wind speed coupled with the small island land mass spun it straight toward South Florida.

It was a direct strike when Wilma made landfall, a Category 3 at 125 mph at 6:30 AM October 24th. Most South Floridians were sleeping and only woke when the electricity and air conditioning cut out. Very few homeowners had put up shutters (again!) or had made emergency preparations. We awoke to flooded streets, power lines were down, fallen trees in people's pools and driveways, missing street signs, and there was no hot coffee for hundreds of miles. The only sound was of garbage cans rolling around amongst the trash that was strewn everywhere. It's funny how eerily silent a community gets with no electricity or traffic. I could go on, but the purpose of this book is to prepare YOU, so the effects of a deadly hurricane don't play out in your lives.

2
WHAT MAKES A STORM A HURRICANE?

HURRICANES ARE UNIQUE in that they can travel across both water and land. You can't outrun a hurricane once it makes landfall. Tornadoes can be embedded within hurricane rain bands although they are usually weak and short-lived. Tornado formation often happens before the eye passes over.

Hurricanes have warm cores, which means the air temperature increases towards the center of the storm. The eyewall is 6-12 miles from the center of the eye and has the highest winds, most torrential rains and the thickest clouds of the hurricane.

Hurricanes rarely last more than 12-18 hours start to finish, once they make landfall. In 2017 Hurricane Irma was the exception to that, lasting 36 hours. She traveled up the center of the state of Florida and took her sweet time.

There are three main types of hurricanes: primarily high winds, primarily heavy rainwater, or a combo of both high winds and heavy rainwater. Hurricanes Katrina in NOLA and Superstorm Sandy in NY/NJ would be examples of a combo of both. When making preparations, it is good to prepare for a combination of both types because even with current sophisticated weather prediction equipment, forecasters still can't tell you what the outcome will be in your locality.

PRIMARILY HIGH WINDS

Mexico Beach, Florida – Hurricane Michael, 2018 Category 5

Hurricane winds and storm surges are most intense on the right-hand side of the storm, relative to the direction of travel. In the Northern hemisphere, hurricane winds travel counter-clockwise. In the center or 'eye' of the storm, there are mostly clear, blue skies. After the eye passes, the wind direction switches and moves powerfully clockwise. During the first half of the storm sustained winds are pulling trees and structures one way.

All through the second half of the storm sustained winds are blowing trees and structures the other way. The second half of the hurricane is when the most damage occurs because structures are weakened during the early hours of the storm.

Once sustained winds pass 74 mph they are assigned a category on the **Saffir-Simpson Hurricane Wind Scale**. Following is each category, and a brief description of what is possible at that sustained wind speed:

Category 1 – 74 to 95 mph

Well-constructed frame homes could have damage to the roof, shingles, vinyl siding, and gutters.

Large branches of trees may snap, and shallowly rooted trees may be uprooted.

Damaged power lines and poles could result in miles-wide power outages that could last from a few to several days.

Category 2 – 96 to 110 mph

Well-constructed frame homes could sustain significant roof and siding damage.

Shallowly rooted trees could be snapped or uprooted and blocking roads.

Power loss is expected with outages that could last from several days to weeks.

Category 3 – 111 to 129 mph

Well-built framed homes may incur significant damage, blown out roof decking, and gable ends.

Many trees will be snapped or uprooted, blocking numerous roadways making car travel impossible.

There will be no electricity and water for several days or weeks after the storm passes.

Category 4 – 130 to 156 mph

Well-built framed homes can sustain severe damage with loss to most of the roof structure and some exterior walls. Most trees will be snapped or uprooted, and power poles downed. Fallen trees and power poles will isolate residential areas. Street signs will be toppled. Power outages will last for several weeks or possibly months. Most of the area will be uninhabitable for weeks or months.

Category 5 – over 157 mph

A high percentage of framed homes will be destroyed, with total roof failure and wall collapse.

Fallen trees and power poles will isolate residential areas. Power outages will last for several weeks or possibly months. Most of the area will be uninhabitable for weeks or months. For reference, lift-off for a jet airliner is 180 MPH.

Check out this simulation for a visual of possible home damages for Categories 1-5:

https://www.youtube.com/watch?v=lqfExHpvLRY

PRIMARILY HEAVY RAINWATER

Houston, Texas - Hurricane Harvey, 2017 Category 4

Ninety percent of hurricane-related deaths are from water. Hurricanes form and strengthen over large bodies of water. As they are churning counterclockwise and moving forward, they are sucking up the water from beneath. Once the hurricane makes landfall, it slows, and the water dumps as rainwater.

Hurricane Florence, a slow-moving Category 1 hurricane dumped over 18 trillion gallons of water over the Carolinas.

Hurricane Harvey, a Category 3 hurricane dumped 33 trillion gallons over Texas and Lousiana. ***Hurricane Lane*** dropped a record 52.2 inches of rain on the Big Island of Hawaii. The Category 3 storm struck on August 24, 2018.

Hurricane Walaka was a Category 5 monster that destroyed the East Island of the Hawaiian chain on October 1, 2018. This island, which is now submerged, was a habitat for endangered Hawaiian monk seals and sea turtles.

If you live in a coastal area, you also need to pay particular attention to the Coastal Flood Watches and Coastal Flood Warnings; they track the storm surge probabilities which is the deadliest part of a hurricane.

Storm surge is an abnormal rise of water generated by the storm's high winds. Storm surge can reach heights of 20 feet and above and can span hundreds of miles of coastline. The expanses of the coast where the ocean floor slopes gradually are the stretches where hurricanes will cause the highest storm surge. This surge can travel several miles inland. Storm surges can also be compounded by the regular tide tables of that coast, causing quick and substantial flooding. This is called a Storm Tide. Much of the United States densely populated Atlantic and Gulf of Mexico coastlines lie less than 10 feet above sea level.

The devastating power of a storm surge coupled with large battering waves can make a storm death toll rise, topple large buildings, produce beach and dune erosion, and cause road and bridge outages along the coast. Hurricane Katrina's storm surge in New Orleans was recorded at 25 to 28 feet above normal tide levels, and her death toll was 1,833.

For a visual storm surge check out this simulation: https://www.youtube.com/watch?v=q01vSb_B1o0

COMBO OF BOTH HIGH WINDS AND HEAVY RAINWATER

If you watch the above two YouTube simulations back to back and think: Hurricanes Katrina and Sandy, you get the idea of what happens when a combination of wind and water devastate a coastline and the cities on it. When the storm surge coincides with high tide, you get storm tide. This occurrence is what created the most devastation during Hurricane Sandy. Water weighs 1,700 pounds per cubic yard. The combined force of the stor and the weight of the water is destructive and dangerous.

Now that I have your attention as to the seriousness of an approaching hurricane, it is time to move on to successful preparations.

Hurricane Katrina, New Orleans, LA

"Is your name on the 'Retired' hurricane name list? How does this happen? We do not control the naming of tropical storms. Instead, a list of names has been established by an international committee of the United Nations World Meteorological Organization. For Atlantic hurricanes, there is one list for each of six years. In other words, one list is repeated every seventh year. The only time that there is a change is if a storm is so deadly or costly that the future use of its name on a different storm would be inappropriate for obvious reasons of sensitivity. If that occurs, then at an annual meeting by the committee (called primarily to discuss many other issues) the offending name is stricken from the list, and another name is selected to replace it. See here for more information: https://www.nhc.noaa.gov/aboutnames_history.shtml"

3
JUNE FIRST; TWELVE ESSENTIAL ACTIONS

IT IS ALWAYS wise to prepare as if the hurricane eye will hit where you live if you happen to live in a hurricane-prone area. Prepare on June first for the complete six-month hurricane season; through November 30th every year, and not just a possible storm as it approaches. Review your homeowners, flood, and automobile policies. Call your agent with any questions you may have about your policies. They make an annual commission from your policy so let them earn it. You'll read in chapter seven that these policies have exclusions that, knowing ahead of time you can prepare for them.

> "Hurricanes have killed more people worldwide in the last 50 years than any other natural cataclysm."
> Kerry Emanuel

Supply your pantry with the nonperishable necessities you would need for five days if you stayed in your house. Determine how much water your household will need for 5-6 days and store it in an air-conditioned place if possible. The **"Storm Cupboard Supply List"** is in Appendix 1. These preparations will save you from those last-minute runs to the grocery and hardware stores, only to find bare shelves when a hurricane is on its way.

☐ **Food:** Preplan five days of meals that can be frozen, then eaten without using a stove or oven. Create a shopping list for these meals, along with the last-minute supplies you will need. Put it in a handy place. When you're in the path of a hurricane, there will be so much mental stimulation coming at you, that you will be glad to have this ready-made list in hand. You'll know when to use it.

- ☐ **Alternative Housing:** Another June first conversation would be to explore ideas for ten-day, and beyond housing options for your family and pets in case you must evacuate. Have a confirmed place to go in the event of a worst-case scenario — to a second home, a relative's home, etc. It's just good sense to have these conversations ahead of the season in case a longer-term emergency plan becomes necessary.

- ☐ **An evacuation plan** is a good conversation to have on June first. It would include planning your route in several different directions, depending on the path of the storm.

- ☐ **Assemble an "Emergency Car Go-Bag"** – See the checklist in Appendix 2

Keep these ***additional*** emergency supplies for ***your house and car*** based on your family's individual needs:

- ☐ Prescription medications
- ☐ Non-prescription medications such as pain relievers, anti-diarrhea medicine, antacids or laxatives
- ☐ Glasses and contact lens solution
- ☐ Mosquito repellant and sunblock
- ☐ Infant formula, bottles, diapers, wipes, diaper rash cream
- ☐ Pet food and extra water for your pet
- ☐ Cash or traveler's checks
- ☐ Important family documents such as copies of insurance policies, identification, and bank account records saved electronically or in a waterproof, portable container
- ☐ Sleeping bag or warm blanket for each person
- ☐ Complete change of clothing appropriate for your climate and sturdy, closed-toe shoes
- ☐ Household chlorine bleach and medicine dropper to disinfect water

Hurricane Preparation and Survival

- ☐ Fire extinguisher
- ☐ Matches in a waterproof container
- ☐ Feminine supplies and personal hygiene items
- ☐ Shaving kit
- ☐ Mess kits, paper cups, plates, paper towels, and plastic utensils
- ☐ Paper and pencil

- ☐ **Your Pet Plan:** June first is also the time when pre-planning for our furry (and not so furry) loved ones is crucial. If you evacuate, plan to take them with you. Many shelters do not accept pets for health and safety reasons. The Red Cross advises that if it is not safe for you to stay at home for the storm, it's not safe for your pets either. Over 250,000 pets went missing during Hurricane Katrina because they were left behind.

Pets and poop - Most likely our furry friends could be held hostage indoors for up to a day and a half. They will need to relieve themselves and may do so whether you provide a place or not. It's a tough call. You can put some sod down in the garage and take them out there.

Make sure your pets have up to date tags and immunizations. To get a free emergency pet alert sticker for your home, go to https://secure.aspca.org/take-action/order-your-pet-safety-pack and allow 6-8 weeks for delivery. Your local pet supply store may also sell similar stickers.

For an "**Emergency Pet Checklist**" see Appendix 5.

- **Hurricane Plan:** Have a family meeting and prepare a detailed "Hurricane Plan" for your family. Everyone's input is important. The "**Simple Hurricane Plan Outline**" is in Appendix 3.

  During the six months of hurricane season, keep an eye on the weather in the oceans nearest you. The hurricanes that hit the east coast of the US and the Gulf of Mexico originate as sandstorms off the coast of Africa. The good news is the storms are usually tracked for ten days to two weeks before a hurricane makes landfall. The bad news is they don't know until one to twelve hours ahead of time precisely where the eye of the hurricane will hit, and by then your power may have gone out. For a visual check this out: https://svs.gsfc.nasa.gov/12772

- **Assemble Necessary Tools**: Prime and start your generator and chainsaw to make sure they are working properly. Decide where you will place the generator and pre-check (or have an electrician) the electrical connections. Also, check and charge any power tools you may need for emergency repairs after the storm. Make sure you have an adequate supply of the proper oils and containers of gasoline for the generator and chainsaw.

- **Plan for Mitigation:** Purchase tarps and fasteners to the dimensions of your roof to have on hand for a worst-case scenario. Per your insurance policy, you are obligated to stop further damage once the storm passes. The weather after a hurricane can be unpredictable, with more wind and rain. From this moment on, keep and file all receipts having to do with anything about your home. Whether it is a towel set from Target or a new generator installed outside your home. Keep the receipts in a safe place, together. If you need to evacuate quickly, you can put them in a Ziplock bag and go. You will need them for your insurance claim.

- **Tradespeople:** As a catastrophic insurance adjuster, the most often asked question I get is 'Who can I get to do the repairs?' The first week in June, make a list of all the tradespeople you know personally and write down their names and numbers. This list would include General Contractors, roofers, plumbers, electricians, flooring companies, Public Adjusters, etc. If you don't know any, now is the time to ask trusted family members and friends for names and references. An excellent resource is firefighters; many have second jobs or businesses in the trades. Finding a trusted Emergency Mitigation Service is also critical. If the inside of your house becomes wet, you may need a dry out service to mitigate any mold or mildew growth (first read AOB in chapter 8).

- **Document everything**
  Photos: On June first walk around the outside of your house, and outside structures and photograph each side separately. On the interior, photograph each room from all four angles, plus the ceiling and floors (closets too). Photograph valuable antiques, artwork and contents separately. If you have a boat or RV, decide where you will secure them. Photograph them from all angles; inside and out. Transfer the photos to a folder on your computer and email them to yourself. Insurance policies: email these documents to yourself too.

- **June One Home Inspection:** As you photograph your house look closely to see if there are places where wind or wind-driven rain could enter. Are there any loose boards, doors, windows or areas that need caulk? Cracked or broken windows? Loose roof tiles or shingles? This is where an ounce of prevention could save you days, even weeks of aggravation and repairs.

Examine and photograph your roof. Is there loose or missing shingles or tiles? If in doubt, hire a roofer to inspect for you. Keep their written report with your insurance papers or receipts. Thinking you'll wait for a hurricane to get a new roof out of your insurance company is delusional. If you end up needing a replacement roof after the storm, the interior of your home could also have severe water damage. In the time it takes to get a new roof (which can be months after a hurricane), and interior repairs in a hurricane hit area, mold will continue to grow in your home. Mold and mildew can cause long term illness in susceptible individuals, children, and older adults.

The National Safety Council outlines ladder safety in the event that you are inspecting your own roof: https://www.nsc.org/home-safety/tools-resources/safety-checkup/ladders

- **Last but NOT Least:** Find and assemble all of your storm shutters and make sure they are well oiled, fit and working properly. Replace any missing hardware. Mark which pieces (even if it is plywood) covers which window or door.

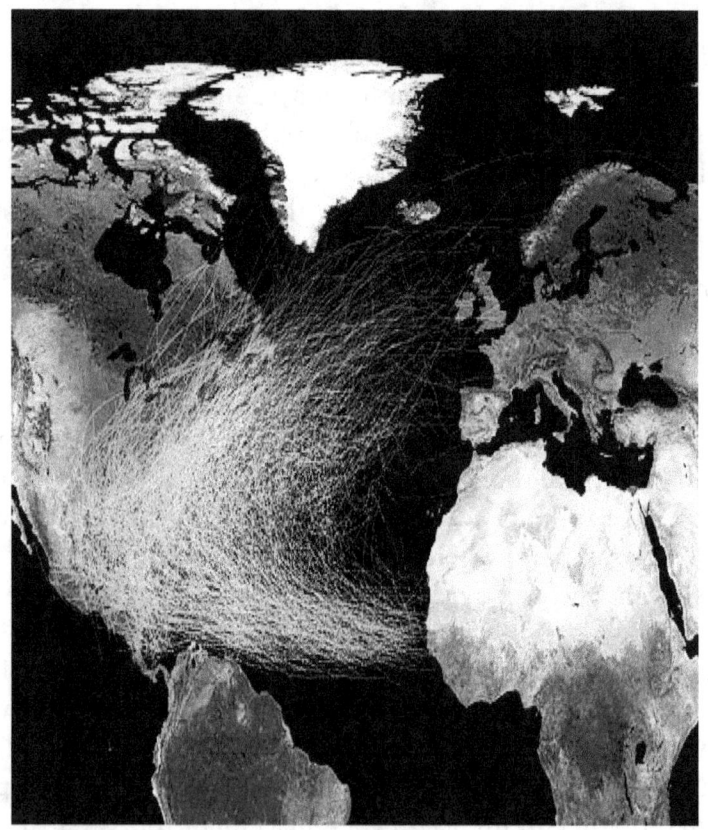

Hurricane Alley - Hurricanes start as dust storms from Africa

4
A TEN DAY TIMELINE FOR AN APPROACHING STORM

Stay or Leave?

LET'S FACE IT; if we evacuated every time we saw a hurricane in the ocean, we would be broke by the end of Hurricane season. So, how do we decide whether to stay, or leave? In all states except Florida, a mass exit is possible on the main roads away from the coast. In Florida evacuating takes more preplanning.

If you do decide to leave ahead of an evacuation order, these are sound recommendations:

- *Five days before landfall* secure your belongings and pack your valuables for transit. Bring games, books, tablets, anything useful for self-entertainment. Gas up.

- *Four days before landfall* bring in all outside items that could blow away, or possibly become a missile in heavy winds. Shutter and board up your windows and doors. Stack valuable and sentimental items on a shelf over six feet high. Leave your contact information with neighbors, and in a waterproof bag taped to the inside of your front window.

- *Two to three days before landfall* turn the key and drive away. You've made your decision for your safety and the safety of your loved ones. Everybody who is leaving will be doing so within this timeframe if they are smart. The road conditions will become slower the closer you get to the predicted hour of landfall. Prepare yourself for possible gasoline lines. Don't be swayed by people who love to give their unsolicited advice and opinions. You are guaranteeing your safety. Go, and enjoy the peace of mind you have planned for yourself. Hopefully, you *will* be wrong and will return to a dry home.

Evacuation tip: Freeze a cup of water solid. When you leave, put a coin on top of the frozen water. When you come back, you will be able to tell if your food went completely bad and refroze, or if it stayed frozen while you were gone. If the coin has fallen to the bottom of the cup that means all the food defrosted and it should be thrown out. Otherwise, it could still be edible.

About shelters ...

> "The first rule of hurricane weather coverage is that every broadcast must begin with palm trees bending in the wind."
> Carl Hiaasen

If you live in a mobile home or low lying coastal area, there may be a mandatory evacuation order from your state and local officials. If you are considering a shelter, know that shelters have their own set of rules. They are not designed for comfort; only safety. Most shelters will only take service animals, and these animals may have to be preregistered well ahead of a hurricane.

For the "Shelter Supply List" see Appendix 4.

What do those SIX warnings TV forecasters keep talking about mean for me?

TROPICAL STORM WATCH - Tropical Storm conditions with sustained winds from 39 -74 mph are possible in your area within the next 36 hours. If at this point, you have committed to staying in your home or the area for the duration of the storm, there is work to do. It's exhausting and kind of exciting, too.

Hurricane Preparation and Survival

During the countdown to expected landfall:

- Remember that meal planning and shopping list? Grab it and go shopping. Begin preparing and freezing these meals. At the very least, the storm will pass you by, and you'll have a few days away from the kitchen.
- Trim coconuts from trees. These become missiles during hurricane force winds.
- Prime and check your generator one last time.
- Charge up portable generators.
- Keep device batteries charged.
- Secure your boat and RV. Fighting with ropes in high winds is never fun.
- Fill your car and generator gas tanks and keep full.
- Help someone else.

TROPICAL STORM WARNING - Tropical Storm conditions are expected in your area within the next 24 hours. If you had decided to leave, you should be getting on the road by the next daylight.

- Bring in loose outdoors objects; lawn chairs, garbage cans, plants, etc.
- Set the refrigerator to coldest setting.
- Decide where all the vehicles will go. Find covered parking in the community, if possible.
- Vacuum, do laundry, and shower if possible. Power outages can last days or weeks.
- Help someone else.

HURRICANE WATCH - Hurricane conditions with sustained winds of 74 mph or greater are possible in your area within the next 36 hours. A hurricane watch should TRIGGER your disaster plan; the one you made ahead on June first and have been discussing amongst yourselves. The final decision to ***stay or leave*** should have been made by now. If local Emergency Managers issue an evacuation order, then you must do so immediately. Only use travel routes specified by local authorities.

Secure your home before leaving. From this point on every family member should know where each other is.

- Buddy up!

HURRICANE WARNING - Hurricane conditions are expected in your area within 24 hours. Once this WARNING has been issued, your family should be completing protective actions, and deciding the safest location inside the house to be during the storm for you and your pets (an interior room, a closet or bathroom on the lower level).

- Fill a large cooler or the washing machine with bags of ice. Fill gallon containers and freeze them for extra ice/water.
- Close the shutters. Do NOT go outside.
- Place towels along the front and back door bottoms, keeping buckets, mops, and rags handy.
- Sanitize the bathtubs with bleach, and fill. If you lose water pressure, you can use this to flush the toilets.
- Collect valuables (computers, jewelry, photographs, etc.) and put on a shelf six feet high.
- Plug a small TV into a portable generator. Have it tuned to the disaster station ahead of time.
- If the power goes out, unplug everything; there could be possible damage from a power surge.
- Place a ladder next to the attic opening, keeping a hatchet handy.

If you live within fifteen miles of any waterway or coast, then you need to also watch for these official warnings:

COASTAL FLOOD WATCH - The possibility exists for flooding of land areas along the coast in the next 12 to 36 hours.

COASTAL FLOOD WARNING - Land areas along the coast are expected to become, or have become, inundated by sea water above the typical tide action.

Double Danger: Storm Tide and Surge

Storm surge is an abnormal rise in the water level that is generated by hurricane winds. It can be well over 25 feet and span hundreds of miles of coastline. Tides are the rise and fall of sea levels caused by gravitational forces exerted by the Moon and Sun, and the rotation of Earth. If you live along a coast, you are probably aware of the lunar tide that comes in and recedes twice a day. This happens approximately fifty minutes later each day.

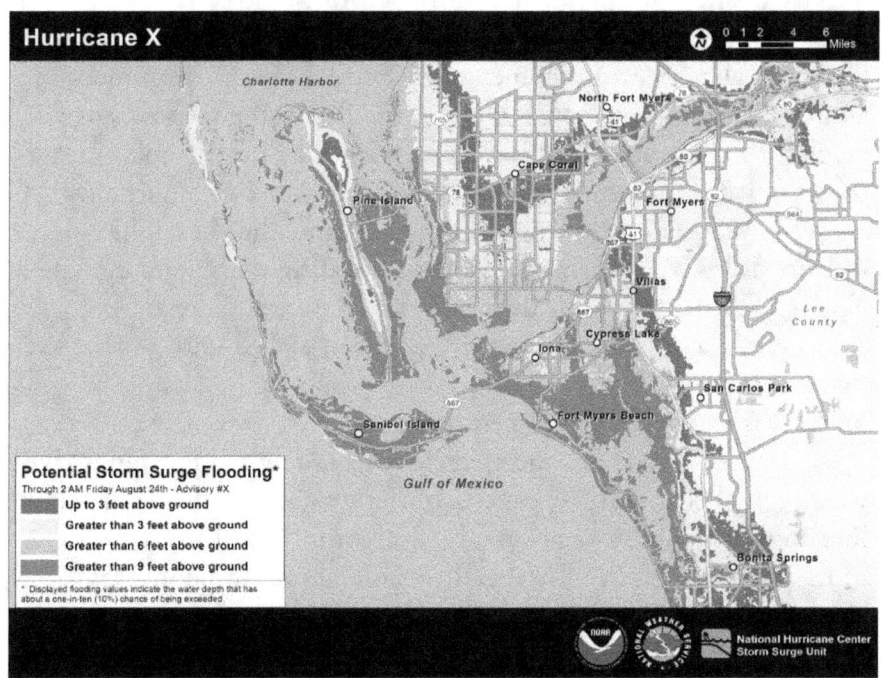

Storm surge map for the Fort Myers, Florida coastline

Another useful chart is a tide chart: http://tides.mobilegeographics.com/locations/698.html

Tides generally vary by three to four feet depending on the lunar cycle. You can couple the ETA of the storm within the tide cycle and see how the two will affect each other. Conditions rapidly deteriorate once the storm is 36 hours away.

Dee and Bill's Hurricane Story — Water and Coastal Surge

Hurricane Irma, September 17th, 2017

"After Hurricane Irma we had to wait two weeks before we could even get into the Keys because all the roads were closed. Only first responders could get past the Florida City checkpoint officials. They had to make sure the bridges were safe, and the roads weren't washed out. They had to fix a lot of roads.

When they finally let us residents in, we took two cars- Bill had loaded up all his work equipment; generators, blowers, dehumidifiers, and chain saws. When we got there, the first thing we saw was our neighbor's aluminum roof laying in our back yard. It took out our two, beautiful, mature queen palm trees. It was a mess out back.

The weather was muggy, 95 degrees and the flies! They were unstoppable. We saw there was more flooding than wind damage. The houses that were on stilts didn't have much damage.

Our place was a mold pit! It had been closed and hot for the two weeks since Irma. We started out wearing breathing masks, but it was way too hot to keep them on.

Our first call was to the electrician. He rewired the plugs. We were lucky because our 220 A/C outlet was above the flood water line so when the power came on, we could plug in our room ac unit. There were lots of house fires from shorts in people's wiring after the storm.

In our 1200 square foot duplex, the doors lining the long carport were ripped off. The washer and dryer and refrigerator had floated away. There was a 33" water line, with sand and debris everywhere. In the kitchen, the pots, pans, and silverware were rusted and full of sand.

We began by shoveling the muck from the rooms. The locals said that the water from the ocean took a long time to build to the 33" water line, and then the water quickly rushed back out to sea.

Bill cut the sheetrock four feet high, pulled the carpets and flooring and dragged it all out to the street. You could see right through the house, from the street to the canal behind us. But in the bedrooms, the beds were made, and the pillows were still sitting pretty, as if nothing ever happened! Our power was not restored until the end of December; the electrician in September just did the wires above the watermarks for the air conditioning wall units to help dry things out.

A Red Cross was opened at the Marathon Key Community Center about three miles north of us. That's where we had to go to get our drinking water, ice and government meal replacements every day. There were no open food stores at that time. The power was restored about a month after the hurricane hit, just in time for my birthday!

Dee: 'My 60th Birthday was 10/21, and we were just into the cleanup. I was totally overwhelmed by the amount of work to be done and lack of help finding a contractor. While in Publix that day, I saw a flyer taped to the wall, "DO YOU NEED HELP?" I took a picture of it and called the number when I got back to my car. It turns out it was some church people sitting in the van right next to me. They asked my age, and I told them 60. They said that I would be moved to the top of their list since I was over 60! They were ten Mormons who called themselves 'Helping Hands Jupiter,' and right then they followed me back to our place. There were ten of them in that van, and the oldest one who was their leader had to be only twenty years old. They helped Bill move appliances, shovel sheetrock, and wheel barreled heavy stuff out to the street for pick up. They even brought their own garbage bags!

The insurance adjuster came 3 or 4 days later and stayed a half day assessing our damages. Citizens paid for 'loss of use' for two weeks.

Every day the garbage trucks came, hauling the contents and debris away. The roads were a mess, and it could take forever to go anywhere if you got stuck behind one of those trucks! Every mile there was a porta potty because there was no power or water service. People were living in tents. Rents were sky high if you were lucky enough to find a place. People who had evacuated were immediately evicted upon their return because their rents had been raised beyond their affordability.

In the middle of all this were the heartwarming efforts of everyday people. There was a Dunkin tent with free coffee; what a lifesaver that was! There were lots of church groups coming down and helping to clean up.

Then the rains came, and it rained for three days. The sewers were full of sand, and everything flooded again, including the roads. For months there was no boating in the Keys because of floating debris, refrigerators and the large appliances that were submerged.

In December the house was once again closed in, and we started painting and decorating. We had terrific, repeat tenants checking in on January 20th and had vowed to have the place ready by then. We bought new appliances from Home Depot and began finding good, used furniture near our home in Deerfield Beach, FL. One week before our tenants were due, we loaded everything up into a moving van and drove back to the Keys.'

When did you begin to feel real hope? Moment of hope was when "Helping Hands, Jupiter" came in to help us, AND finding a contractor.

What was your darkest moment? Our worst moment was just the overwhelming amount of work and lack of help and finding a contractor.

Describe someone who had it a lot worse than you. People south of us had it much worse (if you can imagine) Big Pine Key and Cudjoe had the 'eye' and much more structural damage. At least we had our outside walls and our roof."

"Anyone who says they're not afraid at the time of a hurricane is either a fool or a liar, or a little bit of both."
Anderson Cooper

5
RIDING OUT THE STORM

What to expect and Do:

THE WEATHER WILL tell you when to close and lock all your doors and windows for good. Once you, as a group have committed to this decision, ***do not go outside*** until the hurricane passes. That especially includes the eye. Plug ALL rechargeables in (don't forget your camera battery) possibly one last time for a while.

Each hurricane has its own length of time. There are many variables that factor into this timeframe: the water temperature, the land masses the storm is slamming against, how long the hurricane has been sitting on a body of water strengthening, and its wind speed and size.

Here are the lengths of the duration of recent hurricanes in the USA:

Katrina – 6 hours – 1883 dead
Sandy – 4 hours – 147 dead
Wilma – 4.6 hours – 61 dead
Michael – 4 hours – 48 dead
Irma – 2 days – 102 dead
Andrew – 3.5 hours – 65 dead
Florence – 3 days – 53 dead

The first telling event that the storm has worsened is if/when your power goes out. If you have a generator, you may want to power it up at that time. The existence of the impending storm no longer holds any excitement. The reality of no electricity, no air conditioning, and dark, shuttered windows and doors is a rude awakening. That white blob on every television station that you had been fixated on for days, and come to dislike, has suddenly become a black screen. Poof! You and your neighbors are in the dark; there is no contact and no internet.

Intensifying winds are whipping around your house, sometimes making a howling noise. All exterior sounds become heightened; after all, there is no TV, AC, or Alexa to break the silence. You may hear a garbage can flying down the street and wonder if your one, know-it-all neighbor was smart enough to secure his outdoor furniture before commencing his hurricane party. Or if his lawn chair will implant itself in your car's rear window. The indoor air may become hot and stifling.

If the rain has not begun, it will shortly. Window sills or door bottoms may leak; put towels down to keep the areas dry. Wood and laminate floors are very susceptible to water damage. Paint and drywall can easily become waterlogged. Check regularly for leaks from the roof, putting a bucket down to catch any water. Keep buckets, mops, and rags handy.

About your phone: You'll need at least one phone with a full battery charge for after the storm passes. As much as you'll want to use it, it's a good idea to create a new message such as, "My phone has been turned off to conserve battery power for after the storm. I'll be checking texts at ten AM and six PM, (or whatever times are good for you) and will get back to you if it is an emergency. XXX is my contact person, and we will call them with updates if necessary. Their number is XXX-XXX-XXXX." Then turn off your phone and put it in a room you don't visit often. Addictions are hard to break, and we are surely addicted to our phones! On another note, it might be fun to watch your teen run out of juice. I know, not funny.

Tape the refrigerator door closed, appointing a 'refrigerator guard.' Open it only for meal preparation. Learn to drink room temperature water. You don't know when the electricity will come back on. After Hurricane Wilma, mine was out for seventeen days.

Check your battery-powered radio device once an hour and track the storm as a group.

Track the storm on your hurricane tracking chart: https://www.nhc.noaa.gov/AT_Track_chart.pdf

On the tracking chart notate the new coordinates and connect the dots. Keep the map attached to a central spot such as the refrigerator or blank TV screen.

What NOT to do during a hurricane:

Stay away from windows, skylights, and glass doors.

If flooding threatens your home, turn off electricity at the main breaker.

If you lose power, turn off all electronics and major appliances such as the air conditioner and water heater to reduce damage from a possible power surge.

Do not use electrical appliances, including your computer.

Do not go outside. If the eye of the storm passes over your area, there will be a short period of calm.

At the other side of the eye, the wind speed will rapidly increase to full hurricane force coming from the opposite direction. Also, do not go outside to see "what the wind feels like." It is too easy to be hit by flying debris.

Beware of lightning. Stay away from electrical equipment. Don't take a bath/shower during the storm.

Stay alert to sounds of possible outside events happening to your home, and cars. Again, DON'T GO OUTSIDE even if you hear something crash. You've made it this far, and the end is in sight. It comes quickly.

Unplugged Activities for Adults:

By now you're pretty exhausted from EVERYTHING overload. If it's still daytime bring out your games, books, playing cards and hobbies that don't require electricity. Think outside the box for things to do: write a bucket list, start a blog, organize your room or man cave, experiment with different make-up styles, give yourself a facial, paint your nails different colors, plan a dream vacation, teach your dog a new trick, dress up your dog, start your autobiography in longhand, rearrange the furniture, learn how to make new cocktails, throw out old spices, read a cookbook, sharpen your knives, read your insurance policy. Take a nap and conserve your energy because you will need it once the storm passes.

Entertainment for kids:

Do art projects.

Have a treasure hunt in the house (use flashlights!).

Write down the kids' favorite recipes and make a family recipe book.

Pretend to go camping in the living room or your safe room area.

Play long car ride games in the house, like, "I spy, I spy something..."

Put on a fashion show.

Put on an art show using their art from school, or with art you just created.

Make musical instruments and then create a marching band or play instruments the kids are learning.

Play with balloons.

Do science experiments or engineering projects with marshmallows and toothpicks.

Make paper bag puppets and then put on a puppet show.

Build something with blocks or Legos.

Build puzzles.

Go on a trip and learn geography and culture...with a travel book.

Have a family talk: Go over the best part of their day, the saddest part of their day, and the funniest part of their day.

Go over your emergency communication plan: https://www.ready.gov/make-a-plan

> "The more violent the storm, the quicker it passes."
> Paulo Coelho

Clean and go through closets. It's a great time to organize and purge clothes and old toys.

Lisa's Story: Hurricane Michael: October 16th, 2018

"I live in South Florida and was visiting my family in Tallahassee. The week before Hurricane Michael I left West Palm Beach to go to my grandmother's memorial service and then continue to Tallahassee. I had planned to return the following Thursday. When I left home, there was a storm out there in the Gulf of Mexico. I think it was a tropical depression at the time; a little low-pressure deal on the edge of Mexico. My dad lets me know these things because he works for the Public Service Commission, so when there are weather events that are going to affect you, he knows about them. Before I even left, he said, "There's nothing out there just so you know," being the caring father that he is, and I said, "Oh it's okay, I'm not worried about it, it's so far away." There was some other storm that had just fizzled out right before.

Hurricane Preparation and Survival

By Monday; they were saying, "Oh it's a category one." I don't remember the exact timeline, but it was early in the week, and it was still a low-grade storm. There wasn't a whole lot of concern and no one expected it to get stronger. I was staying with my brother, and as far as preparing, we knew by the beginning of the week that it was going to be OK. There was going to be a storm and we would make sure that we'd be kind of ready. Realistically we still had about four for five days to prepare.

Two days later we were saying, "Oh there's a storm we should actually, maybe care about. Let's put a few things together because, with us Floridians, that's the way it kind of goes." We think, "Oh, we don't need to worry about it until we realize that it's actually become a more interesting storm. Again, you don't know which way it is going to go. It could always go a little more east or west. Tallahassee is in kind of this weird pocket of no-mans-land when it comes to storms. I don't know why, but in that part of the coast of the Panhandle, where it goes into the armpit of Florida, not many hurricanes ever come through. They either stay south and hit central and south Florida, or they'll go farther west and hit Pensacola or Panama City. Our pocket of Florida, in my lifetime has not seen much action. We do get storms, but it's always the fringe or the edges.

I got concerned because I was supposed to be leaving on Thursday so I could be at work on Friday. At that point, I started thinking, "Should I leave? Should I stay?" I wanted to stay; obviously, I wanted to be with my friends and family, but then I thought, "I don't know what this storm is going to do. If it goes further South, I'll get stuck in traffic with everyone evacuating and have a gas crisis because everyone's freaking out. Then I'll be stuck in the middle of I-75, in the middle of a hurricane." I decided that I was going to stay in Tallahassee and ride it out. I could always make another decision later because in a few hours I'd know something more.

I wasn't scared, I but I was nervous because I wasn't sure if I was making the right decision. My family hadn't decided at that point what they would do either. No one talked about evacuating. Tuesday was when we started saying, "Let's bring stuff inside."

At that point, it was too late to decide to leave. I was staying put and anyone who was going to evacuate needed to do it now. Monday night was pretty much the cutoff if people were going to leave. People farther west of Tallahassee had already been told they needed to evacuate because Hurricane Michael had started getting stronger, a category 3. Late on Tuesday, it became a category 4, and by Wednesday, it was a category 5.

My grandmother lives in Tallahassee in a brick house, and she doesn't travel. My parents were staying with her, so that was settled. I stayed with my brother and his family. All the projections were still saying it was going to go farther West, and as time went on the projections moved a little bit more east, closer to us.

In the middle of the afternoon on Wednesday, it got very dark. There was still power; we expected it to go out at some point but were not sure when. We were halfway through the storm, and the wind had started picking up. We were watching out the window the whole time.

In the Florida panhandle the pine trees are different from the south Florida pine trees. In the south, the pine trees are shorter, and they taper off towards the top, and they branch out a lot more. The pines have more bendy, curvy shapes to them, whereas north Florida pine trees grow a lot taller. They are very stiff and straight the whole way up, like a thick telephone pole. In hurricane winds, the entire tree snaps and falls. It's not just a branch that will fall off, so when the trees broke in half, it was loud and devastating. The trees are 50 feet tall and if it's a tree falling, it's a whole tree.

My brother was pacing because he was getting very nervous. Now we couldn't do anything because the power had gone out, and it was dark. He has kids, so he was worried about his kids. At some point, we decided that we needed to stop sitting by the window and watching the hurricane because things were happening all around. Things were falling from the sky, from really high up and making crashing sounds. We heard booms from transformers blowing and flying things knocking poles over and hitting other people's houses.

My nephew is four years old, and knew what was going on, but he was just bored. "Why are there no toys, and why is there no power? I want to play with the things that I can't." My niece didn't understand why we had to conserve cell phone power. She wanted to play video games on the cell phone, so there is that kind of stuff going on during the storm itself. My brother checked the canned goods to make sure we had food, and we had all these leftovers from the memorial in the pantry. There was very minimal food preparing.

We were getting the outer bands of strong wind and rain. It wasn't the outermost bands, but it wasn't the eyewall either. We were somewhere in the middle. The Northeast side of a storm is the worst part of the storm, so that's where we were, northeast part. At some point, we heard a crack. Then there was a big loud bang. Then a significant vibration to the house and the wall against the garage shook. Some stuff that was hanging on the wall fell off. I walked into the garage from the inside door and saw a branch sticking through the roof the garage into the trunk of my sister in law's car.

My brother didn't realize anything had happened. I told him, "You have a hole in your roof. A tree just went through the roof of the garage." A branch had skewered through the car trunk. There was a bunch of outside roof debris on the car. That same branch had also hit my brother's car outside. Then we heard a crash and shattering glass on the other side of the garage door. We went out to investigate after it calmed down a little. My brother and I are just stupid.

It was still relatively early in the storm. We went out to my brother's car because we had to go around the side of the garage.

That's when we saw that a branch had fallen and taken out the back window of his hatchback and one his tail lights. His car was super old, and his wife wanted a reason to get rid of it anyway. He couldn't drive the car around with a tarp on the back, and it wouldn't be worth getting fixed.

After we went back inside, there was stuff crashing all around outside. We could see from my brothers' porch, and we saw a large branch fall and hit my car. A whole tree was laying over the back end of my car! The engine was fine. I remembered that since I had just come from my grandmother's memorial service, I had a bunch of her old family photos stored in my trunk. My thought was that I couldn't let that stuff get wet, and it was raining in the trunk because now there was a big hole in my car. My brother and I had to get the garage door open because it was closer to my car trunk. We got it partially open and rolled underneath to reach through to the trunk window. There was glass everywhere. We finally pulled all of the family photo albums out of the hatchback.

I wanted to cry because I loved my car; it was an extension of myself. I'd had that car since I started college in 2009, almost ten years. It was paid off. I had a lot of memories in that car; lots of conversations, verything meaningful that happened to me had happened in that car. Lots of road trips, ridiculous things, so it was sad.

In the afternoon it got very dark and lasted into the night. The worst of the hurricane lasted an hour or two, and by that time it was night time, so we just went to bed and hoped for the best because there was nothing anyone could do. It was dark and you couldn't see what was going on outside.

In the morning we walked outside to see what everything looked like. In the backyard, there was stuff everywhere, tree branches, debris, objects skewered into the ground that were sticking straight out. The neighbor's tree was the one that fell and hit my brother's roof. Part of it went through the roof, broke on the edge of my brother's house, and then rolled down onto my car. We spent much of Thursday trying to haul pieces of that tree to the edge of the road.

My brother and his wife and I worked, cleaning up the house and the yard. He got on the roof to assess the damage and pulled the tree out of the hole in the roof. I picked up all the glass from my broken car window, and his car that was all over the ground. The kids were trying to run around and play, but there was broken glass everywhere.

I had called the insurance company the day before when my car got hit, in the middle of the hurricane. I said, "Hey I'm in the middle of hurricane Michael, and a tree just fell in my car. I'm making a claim now, and I want to know what to do to get this processed." That morning my parents drove up from my grandmother's house to pick me up, so we could get a rental car for me.

Trying to get across town was slow. The roads had been cleared on one side; you could only drive on that one side. It was a one lane traffic situation. On the major roads, only one of the six lanes had been cleared for travel. Power lines were hanging on the ground and were all over the place. Everything was broken. The whole city of Tallahassee was out of power at that point.

I didn't know if the car rental place would be open, but we had to try. We couldn't call them because all the phone batteries were dying at this point, and we were not able to charge them because there was no power anywhere.

The rental place was open and functioning without air conditioning, and everybody was wearing regular clothes; no uniforms, and they were running the business out of a van in the back. That's how are they were getting power to do business; they just kept the van running. They had a Square with an iPad which they had plugged into the AC adapter on the van in order to charge my debit card for the rental. Another person was taking a nap in the back of the van.

I rented a car and the next day left to go back home in South Florida.

"Hurricane season brings a humbling reminder that, despite our technologies, most of nature remains unpredictable."
Diane Ackerman

6
SURVIVAL IN CRISIS MODE

I WISH I could say a hurricane was like a bad movie that, when it ends, everything returns to normal when you leave the building. This scenario just isn't so. At the very least a hurricane will inconvenience you because there is no electricity right away for many people. That means no hot coffee, hot shower, or hot meals until your power kicks in. The first impulse once the winds have quieted, and the rain has almost stopped, is to go outside and walk around.

There are rules!

<u>Wear rubber boots.</u> If there is any flooding, even minor, there could be live power lines. Standing water may contain hidden, downed power lines. Snakes, rats, and spiders are actively looking for new homes. Fecal matter or toxins from who-knows-where may be in the standing water. Proceed with caution and keep your loved ones inside until you give the all-clear.

<u>Protect and seal your house from further damage and keep the doors closed.</u>

<u>Carefully monitor your pets when they are outside.</u> Debris and other harmful materials may be in your yard. If there is a boil water alert, make sure to boil your pet's water too.

<u>With your camera,</u> walk around the outside of your house photographing everything, even if there is no damage. If there is damage, take full views and close-ups of the area.

Don't drink tap water: boil water for one minute or use eight drops of bleach per gallon; let stand for thirty minutes. Repeat if the water is still cloudy.

Use repellant at dawn and dusk because the mosquitos and flies will be swarming. Find any places outdoors where there is standing water and dump it. Mosquitoes only need a tablespoon of water to breed. Don't forget your sunscreen.

Call the people on your hurricane list and let them know how you are, and that you are alive. Ask them to call others so you can conserve your cell battery power. Plug in your hardline telephone if you have one. It may work.

Open the windows and air your home out.

String a clothesline because you will need a spot to dry your towels, rags, etc. Hurricanes are wet so having a dry-out area is important.

Don't go out in the dark.

Vehicle Safety at this time is crucial! Drive slowly. Do not drive through flooded areas. Six inches of water can cause a vehicle to lose control or possibly stall. A foot of water will float many cars. Be aware of areas where floodwaters have receded. The roads may have weakened and could collapse under the weight of a vehicle. It is possible the hurricane could impact the physical stability of the roadway. Avoid overpasses, bridges, power lines, signs, and other hazards. If there is an explosion that makes it difficult to control your car, immediately pull over, stop the car and set the parking brake. If a power line has fallen on your car, you could be at risk of electrical shock. Stay inside until a trained person can remove the wire.

Help your neighbor.

Electricity is usually not restored right away so expect your coffee, shower and tap water to be cold.

Round up your battery-powered radios and flashlights and recheck the batteries. Replace them periodically as necessary.

After hours of doing nothing while the storm raged away, it's natural to want to DO something. Channel that energy into yard cleanup. Separate debris into piles: Yard debris, building debris, regular garbage, and trash.

7
THREE TYPES OF INSURANCE

THIS TOPIC IS as individual as the storm you may weather. The decisions you made when you purchased your policy will come into play when you make a claim. *Note*: Insurance companies monitor the weather and in order to prevent a wave of insurance claims, they no longer issue new or upgraded coverage (auto, homeowners or commercial business) once a hurricane's path is announced.

About your homeowner's insurance policy (these are general commentaries not meant to supersede the language in your individual policy): Read it, please. In a separate account, if possible, sock away the dollar amount needed for your Hurricane Deductible. This amount is written in **BOLD** type on the first few pages of your policy. To be clear, all deductibles are the amounts you agreed to pay for the necessary repairs to your home and cars. After the amount of your hurricane deductible, you purchased insurance to pay for the rest of the expenses which include damages to your dwelling, other structures, contents and loss of use. Loss of use is defined as *additional* expenses of living away from your damaged home.

After your homeowner's insurance claim is processed the insurance company will send you two your benefit check. The amount will be the amount of the repairs minus depreciation, minus your deductible. If you purchased recoverable depreciation, then the benefit check would be the amount of repairs minus your deductible.

What that looks like is this: You needed a new roof, and the insurance adjuster came up with a figure of $27,000. Your old roof is X number of years old, so the depreciation value is $9,000. The check the insurance company will send you would total $18,000 ($27,000 - $9,000), then minus your hurricane deductible. Your hurricane deductible is different from your regular deductible and much higher; usually 2-5% of the insured value of your home. Let's say your house is valued at $300,000. Two percent of that would be $6,000. The $18,000 roof benefit amount, minus your deductible of $6,000 would equal $12,000. That would be the amount of the check from an insurance company. Again, every policy is written differently, and the above example paints a broad picture. The takeaway is to have your hurricane deductible amount in a separate savings account.

About your flood insurance policy: Flood insurance is a separate policy that can be purchased from your insurance agent or broker. It is written through the National Flood Insurance Program (NFIP) which is managed by the Federal Emergency Management Program (FEMA). According to the NFIP the average flood policy costs $700 per year.

The flood policy consists of two coverages: **Contents** coverage is determined at Actual Cost Value (ACV): the costs to replace damaged or lost goods based on its actual, depreciated value as used goods. Your **Property** coverage can be purchased at ACV or you can purchase Replacement Cost Value (RCV): the costs to replace the damaged or lost property with NEW property without regard to depreciation.

If you live in a high-risk flood zone your mortgage lender will require that you purchase flood insurance. If you live in a low to moderate risk area you don't have to purchase flood insurance for your lender's sake. You may want to purchase it anyways since according to FEMA 25% of all flood claims come from these areas. Also, the official 'risk' designation for floods may be out of date (a common problem). If this is the case the good news is, if you are in a low to moderate risk area your flood insurance will probably be less than $150 a year.

FYI a flood policy covers water that comes from outside your home (only) and the water must have covered at least two acres or have affected at least one other property. If your home sustains any mold or mildew damage that could have been prevented, your flood policy won't cover this damage.

Some items a flood does not cover are flower beds, vegetable gardens, trees, landscaping or damages from a swimming pool leak. Any home improvements made to your basement, or personal property located in basements or other areas of your home located below the lowest elevated floor are not covered by a flood policy. Flood policies also don't cover living expenses, financial losses caused by business interruption, or any other loss of your home's use.

Lastly, a flood policy won't cover the value of any currency, precious metals, stock certificates or other valuable papers that get destroyed in a flood.

Risk Rating 2.0 — in 2020 FEMA is revamping the flood insurance program. Premiums will be based on how close a dwelling is to the coastline and how much it would cost to replace it. Besides proximity to water, FEMA could consider elevation, the number of trees in a neighborhood or the age of storm drains on a given street. The updated program is scheduled to go into effect in October 2020 and does not have to be approved by Congress. For updates refer to the FEMA website.

AN IMPORTANT NOTE ABOUT FLOOD INSURANCE: Flood insurance coverage doesn't kick in until thirty days after you first purchase it. If you are considering flood insurance, June first would be a good time to purchase it.

About your automobile insurance policy: The portion of your auto policy that covers damage by natural events is the comprehensive portion of your car insurance policy. Policies differ but generally comprehensive is designed to cover the car if electronic components are destroyed by water or flood, the car is damaged by falling trees or debris, hail, or is flipped by strong winds or gusts.

When it's safe to go outside take photos from all four sides and close-ups of any damage or objects laying on the car. If it looks as if the damage is above your deductible amount (again, this is the amount you agreed to pay for an occurrence), then call your insurance company to begin a claim.

Your insurer will have you take steps to prevent further loss such as covering smashed windows or tarping open areas of your auto. If you neglect to mitigate these further losses, your auto insurance company could deny coverage. This is written into your policy.

If you elected Rental Car Reimbursement to be sure to find out the coverage limits for it before leaving the rental agency. You will need a valid credit card and driver's license to rent a car.

The final piece of information for most people who have not been through the hurricane insurance claim process is that the checks from the insurance companies are co-written to you, and the lending company who holds your mortgage/automobile. Technically you both own them. Call the lender(s) and ask what the steps are to cash the checks from your insurance company. It's usually quite simple, but it is an unexpected extra step during a financially stressful time.

8
REBUILDING DAMAGED HOMES

Don't Sign Anything until you understand what an AOB is!

AOB = Assignment of Benefits to a third party for work being performed. This means the check the insurance company would send to YOU for repairs will be written to this third party instead. After a hurricane, there are a lot of unsavory companies that do shoddy work. They know the drill and seem to crawl out of the woodwork. Unfortunately, they will have you sign the AOB before they even begin repairs. Beware! Refer to the list of reputable contractors that you researched on June first.

Insurance Adjusters, Public Adjusters and EMS – Who are they?

The insurance adjuster assigned by your insurance company (this could be through a third party independent adjusting firm) will come out to your home and assess the damages. The damages will be photographed and documented, and the adjuster will then write up an estimate of repairs using a cost estimating program that is up-to-date and accurate based on the current pricing and availability of goods per your zip code.

This report is then reviewed and approved by your insurance company. Your benefit check (minus your hurricane deductible, and depreciation) is then sent to the address you provided to your adjuster at the time of the inspection. If your final receipts total more than the benefit, then you can contact the insurance company for a Supplement Claim.

I have found most insurance companies want to help their clients as much as possible from the beginning to the end of your claim. They will work with you.

A public Adjuster (PA) can be a good option if you are completely overwhelmed, sick, elderly, living in another home, or just not able to go through the insurance claims process. Or you may feel your assigned insurance adjuster is not qualified to assess your damages and may want to hire your own adjuster. For a percentage of your total insurance benefit (10%-15%) a PA will evaluate and document your losses. They will also write up an estimate of repairs and present it to you as to what they can get the insurance company to pay. You must sign a contract (an AOB) with them before they begin working for you. If your insurance benefits check is less than you end up needing to rebuild, then the Public Adjuster will also write the supplement claim for you.

Beware! Check out at least three references for the PA you are considering. I have worked with many good, reputable PA's. I have also worked with many who were as crooked as a dog's hind leg. Desperate times are when the scammers come knocking at your door (many *do* go door to door). They may use estimating software that inflates the benefit you would receive from your insurance company. They may print up a stunning grand-total dollar amount of benefits that you 'should' receive from your insurance company. Unsavory PA estimators will add in unnecessary overhead and profit; then DON'T subtract out the hurricane deductible, depreciated amounts AND their commission from this lovely number. They may also recommend their friends (roofers, Emergency Mitigation Services, tradesman) who may, or may not have your best interests at heart.

Reputable Public Adjusters will have references and a website with more than one informational page and will have experience with more than one type of catastrophe. For a good example check out: www.rdadjusting.com

EMS, or Emergency Mitigation Services are the folks who come and dry out the inside of your house after it becomes wet from rainwater or storm surge. Dryout insures there is no mold growth now, or in the future. Again, use a trusted source and check out their references.

Florida's Department of Financial Services advises:

"Understand What You Are Signing During Hurricane Recovery. The Florida Insurance Commissioner warns Floridians recovering from Hurricanes to use caution when asked to sign any paperwork. You could be signing an Assignment of Benefits (AOB). An AOB transfers the insurance claims rights or benefits of your insurance policy to a third party, and it may be presented to a homeowner before repair work begins.

> *Insurance Commissioner:* "Hurricane Michael left widespread devastation in its wake, and as a result, our residents are in a vulnerable state of mind. Homeowners must remain vigilant, review any documents they are asked to sign and use caution when signing an AOB. Consumers can always file a claim directly with their insurance company to maintain control of the rights and benefits provided by their insurance policy throughout their recovery."
>
> *Florida Chief Financial Officer:* "Many of our neighbors in Florida's panhandle lost everything a week ago to Hurricane Michael, and the last thing they need is complications during the rebuilding process. When approached by contractors, homeowners must be cautious if asked to sign any financial paperwork, including an AOB. In some cases, AOB's can delay the claims process and your recovery. ***Be sure to read everything and understand what you are signing before you give away your rights as a homeowner.***"

After assessing damage to your home, restoration professionals may encourage homeowners to sign an AOB. By doing so, you are giving a vendor the right to exclusively communicate with your insurance company, negotiate and endorse insurance claim payments, and potentially file a lawsuit against the insurance company with or without your knowledge.

Remember: after a Hurricane, it can be a total money grab from the insurance companies by restoration and rebuilds services. In the end, YOU will be footing the final bill.

The Florida Insurance Commission gives these following tips to assist during the recovery process:

- Read your insurance policy and understand what your responsibilities are following a loss.
- Contact your insurance company before signing any document that may contain an AOB.
- If you decide to sign the AOB, read everything carefully and do not feel pressured to sign it. Remember, signing an AOB is **not** your only option.
- Beware of language that allows all proceeds of the claim to be made to anyone other than the homeowner or the homeowner's mortgage company.
- Do not sign the document if there are any blank spaces.
- Homeowners should contact their insurance agent, insurance company or Chief Financial Officer Insurance Consumer Helpline in your state for assistance when making repairs after a storm.
- For more information, please visit your states Assignment of Benefits webpage, or read the Office of Insurance Regulation's AOB Resources for your state. The links here are for Florida but the information can apply anywhere.

9
USEFUL APPS FROM YOUR APP STORE

HURRICANE TRACKER

HURRICANE AMERICAN RED CROSS

NOAA NOW

ZELLLO

SNAPCHAT'S SNAP MAP

GASBUDDY

FEMA

CROWDSOURCE RESCUE

HARMANY: AIRBNB BUT MADE SPECIFICALLY FOR SHORT-TERM SHELTER DURING NATURAL DISASTERS

FIRECHAT: NO CELL SERVICE? NO WIFI? NO PROBLEM.

MY HURRICANE TRACKER & ALERTS

WHATSAPP

MAX MAYFIELD'S HURRICANE TRACKER

GLOSSARY & ACRONYMS

American GFS model: Global Forecast System storm model run by the National Weather Service that predicts a storm's projected path

AOB: Assignment of Benefits. An AOB transfers the insurance claims rights or benefits of your insurance policy to a third party, and it may be presented to a homeowner before repair work begins

CONUS: Continental United States

DAC: Disaster Assistance Center

DAE: Disaster Assistance Employee

DFO: Disaster Field Office

Direct Hit: A close approach of a Hurricane to a specific location

Doppler Radar: Radar that measures speed and direction of the wind

EAS: Emergency Alert System

EBS: Emergency Broadcast System

EOC: Emergency Operations Center

EOP: Emergency Operation Plan

ERT: Emergency Response Team

European Model: Model considered by meteorologists to be the most accurate model for predicting hurricanes in the mid-latitudes

Eye: The eye is the circular center of the storm. It is the calmest place in a hurricane since conditions are bright with light winds usually less than 15 mph. The eyewall cloud surrounds it.

Eyewall/ Wall Cloud: An organized band of clouds that surround the eye.

FAST: Field Assessment Team

FEMA: Federal Emergency Management Agency

FCO: FEMA Coordinating Officer

FRP: Federal Response Plan

The Fujiwhara Effect: The effect that occurs when two tropical cyclones orbit around one another

Rain Bands: long, arching bands of clouds and thunderstorms that spiral out from the eyewall

Gale Warning: A warning of one-minute sustained winds in the range of 39 mph to 54 mph.

High Wind Warning: One-minute sustained surface winds of 40 mph lasting for one hour or longer.

Hurricane: A tropical cyclone with winds of 74 MPH or higher.

Indirect Hit: Locations that do not experience a direct hit by a hurricane but experience hurricane force winds and/or tides of at least four feet above normal.

Inundation: The flooding of usually dry land, primarily caused by hurricanes along coasts, estuaries, and rivers.

KM: Kilometers

KT: Knots

Landfall: The intersection of the eyewall with a coastline.

Loss of Use: Insurance coverage that includes the dollar amount of any _additional_ living expenses, meaning any necessary expense that exceeds what you normally spend.

Major Hurricane: A hurricane classified as a Category 3 or higher.

Maximum Sustained Winds: The standard measure of a tropical cyclone's intensity. It refers to the highest one-minute average wind speed.

MB: Millibars

Millibar: A metric unit of air pressure measurement. The average atmospheric pressure at sea level is 1013 millibars. The lower this number goes during a hurricane, the stronger the hurricane becomes.

MPH: Miles per hour

National Hurricane Center: (NHC) National Weather Service office in Coral Gables, FL, that tracks and forecasts hurricanes and other weather in the Atlantic, Gulf of Mexico, Caribbean Sea, and parts of the Pacific.

NM: Nautical mile

NOAA: National Oceanic and Atmospheric Administration

Present Movement: The best estimate of the movement of the center, or eye at a certain time and certain position.

Rapid Intensification: A dramatic increase in the maximum sustained winds of a hurricane.

RD: Regional director

SCO: State coordinating officer

SITREP: Situation report

Supplemental Claim: Payment made based on your insurance company's original estimate of your damages. If this amount is more than the initial payment on your **claim**, you file for a **supplement** to cover the difference.

TD: Tropical depression

TS: Tropical storm

Storm Surge: Quickly rising ocean water levels associated with hurricanes that can cause widespread flooding. Storm surge and large waves produced by hurricanes pose the greatest threat to life and property along the coast.

Storm Tide: The water level rise during a storm due to the combination of storm surge and the astronomical tide.

Tropical Cyclone: A general term for warm weather storm systems that occur over tropical waters, such as tropical storms, hurricanes, and typhoons.

Tide: Tides are the rise and fall of sea levels caused by gravitational forces exerted by the Moon and Sun and the rotation of Earth.

Typhoon: A tropical cyclone that forms in the Pacific Ocean with winds of 74 mph or higher. Typhoons are the same weather phenomena as hurricanes; the only difference between them is the location where the storm occurs.

WFO: Weather forecast office

WRF: Weather research and forecast model

Resources:
https://www.ready.gov/be-informed

APPENDIX 1
"STORM CUPBOARD' SUPPLY LIST"

Do not lend; instead offer to help.

- ☐ $750. cash
- ☐ First Aid kit and manual.
- ☐ Chain Saw (hard hat, goggles, gloves, shoes, tight clothes.) and special fuel.
- ☐ Chain saw and generator manuals in plastic bags.
- ☐ Hand saw (8 or 10 point) and pruners (limb saw).
- ☐ Generator cover and lock, hard wire to the house.
- ☐ Shovel
- ☐ Claw hammer
- ☐ Push broom
- ☐ Screwdriver
- ☐ Pliers
- ☐ Vice grips
- ☐ Utility knife
- ☐ Trash bags
- ☐ Rope
- ☐ Duct tape
- ☐ Extension cords
- ☐ 15 gallons of gasoline, oil
- ☐ 2 tanks of propane
- ☐ 4 large flashlights
- ☐ Extra batteries
- ☐ 2 -5-gallon jugs of water
- ☐ Fan

- ☐ Canned, dry and pet foods
- ☐ Bottled water
- ☐ Dry matches
- ☐ Ice chest
- ☐ Heavy duty plastic bags
- ☐ Bleach, Peroxide, medicine dropper
- ☐ Toilet Paper and paper towels
- ☐ Throwaway camera
- ☐ Paper plates, bowls, napkins, towels, and plastic eating utensils
- ☐ Manual can opener
- ☐ Rain gear, shoes
- ☐ Hardline telephone
- ☐ Extra set of eyeglasses
- ☐ Tarps, furring strips, and nails
- ☐ Cotton work gloves
- ☐ Cleaning supplies
- ☐ Repellant
- ☐ Sunblock
- ☐ Rubber Boots

Power tools may be useless after the storm until the power is restored.

APPENDIX 2
"EMERGENCY CAR GO-BAG" READY FOR TRAVEL

- ☐ One gallon of water per person per day for at least three days, for drinking and sanitation
- ☐ Food - at least a three-day supply of non-perishable food
- ☐ Battery-powered or hand crank radio and an NOAA Weather Radio with tone alert
- ☐ Flashlight
- ☐ First Aid Kit
- ☐ Extra batteries
- ☐ Whistle to signal for help
- ☐ Moist towelettes, garbage bags and plastic ties for personal sanitation
- ☐ Basic, small tool kit
- ☐ Manual can opener for food
- ☐ Local maps
- ☐ Cell phone with chargers and a backup battery
- ☐ Jumper cables
- ☐ Flares or reflective triangle
- ☐ Car cell phone charger
- ☐ Blankets
- ☐ Map
- ☐ Cat litter or sand for better tire traction in case you get stuck

Keep these additional emergency supplies for your house and car based on your family's individual needs:

- ☐ Prescription medications

- [ ] Non-prescription medications such as pain relievers, anti-diarrhea medicine, antacids or [ ] [ ] Laxatives
- [ ] Glasses and contact lens solution
- [ ] Mosquito repellant and sunblock
- [ ] Infant formula, bottles, diapers, wipes, diaper rash cream
- [ ] Pet food and extra water for your pet
- [ ] Cash or traveler's checks
- [ ] Important family documents such as copies of insurance policies, identification, and bank Account records saved electronically or in a waterproof, portable container
- [ ] Sleeping bag or warm blanket for each person
- [ ] Complete change of clothing appropriate for your climate and sturdy, closed-toe shoes
- [ ] Household chlorine bleach and medicine dropper to disinfect water
- [ ] Fire extinguisher
- [ ] Matches in a waterproof container
- [ ] Feminine supplies and personal hygiene items
- [ ] Shaving kit
- [ ] Mess kits, paper cups, plates, paper towels, and plastic utensils
- [ ] Paper and pencil

APPENDIX 3
"HURRICANE PLAN OUTLINE"

http://www.nhc.noaa.gov/refresh/graphics_at4+shtml/085712.shtml?tswind120#contents

Hurricane tracking map: https://www.thoughtco.com/find-best-hurricane-tracking-charts-3443940

Simple Hurricane Plan:

Out of town message relay phone numbers and names:

1.) _____
2.) _____
3.) _____

Buddy System:

_____ is with _____ at all times
_____ is with _____ at all times
_____ is with _____ at all times
_____ is with _____ at all times

If separated, we will meet at (name, address and their phone number) _____ (All names) _____ must be accounted for at all times from the beginning of any **HURRICANE WARNING** until twelve hours after the power is restored. **All phones are kept on a charger and turned on as much as possible during those times.** *Text messages often go through when cell service does not.*

Try to finish the outdoor chores before the rain starts:

HURRICANE WATCH ISSUED

- ☐ Trim coconuts and dead branches from trees. These become missiles during hurricane force winds.
- ☐ Photograph house and assets including the roof.
- ☐ Prepare and freeze food portions (lasagna, cheese cornbread, soup, water for ice, etc.).
- ☐ Generator primed and checked.
- ☐ Gasoline tanks (car and generator) filled and kept full.
- ☐ Charge up a portable generator.

TROPICAL STORM WARNING ISSUED

- ☐ Bring in loose outdoors objects; lawn chairs, garbage cans, plants, etc.
- ☐ Set refrigerator to coldest setting.
- ☐ If evacuating, notify neighbors, family members of the plan. Leave phone numbers.
- ☐ Collect valuables (computers, jewelry, photographs, etc.) put in high, dry place.
- ☐ Decide where all vehicles will go. Find covered parking in the community if possible.
- ☐ Vacuum, do laundry, and shower (wash hair!) if possible. Power outages can last days or weeks.
- ☐ Help someone else.

OUTLASTING THE STORM

- ☐ Close the shutters. Do NOT go outside.
- ☐ Place towels along the front and back door bottoms with buckets, mops, and rags handy.
- ☐ Sanitize bathtub with bleach and fill. Use the water for flushing the toilets if you lose water pressure.
- ☐ Fill the washing machine with ice for a handy cooler.

- ☐ Put important papers and photos including Insurance info into a watertight case.
- ☐ Plug small TV into a portable generator.
- ☐ If the power goes out, unplug everything in the case of damage from a surge.
- ☐ Designate 'safe space' in the house, pets too.
- ☐ Place ladder set next to the attic opening; hatchet is inside opening (remember Katrina).

AFTER THE STORM

- ☐ Don't drink tap water: boil 1 minute or use eight drops bleach per gal, let stand 30 minutes. Repeat if water is still cloudy.
- ☐ Treat all downed power lines as if they are alive with an electrical current.
- ☐ Standing water may have hidden downed power lines, keep out. Don't go out in the dark.
- ☐ Poisonous snakes are homeless, need a home. Keep the doors closed! Brown spiders too! Rats!
- ☐ Protect and seal the house from further damage.
- ☐ Take after pictures, inventory.
- ☐ Separate debris into yard debris, building debris, regular garbage, and trash.
- ☐ Use repellant at dawn and dusk.
- ☐ Plug in a hardline telephone if you have one.
- ☐ Dry everything possible, check for wet areas, dump standing water **everywhere** *(mosquito breeding)*.
- ☐ Help someone else.

APPENDIX 4
"SHELTER SUPPLY LIST"

for 3 to 5 days

- ☐ Drinking water
- ☐ Canned food
- ☐ Manual can opener
- ☐ Prescription medicine
- ☐ Eating utensils, paper plates
- ☐ First aid kit
- ☐ Trash bags
- ☐ Cash
- ☐ Pillows and blankets
- ☐ Sleeping bags
- ☐ Battery operated weather radio
- ☐ Extra batteries
- ☐ Flashlights
- ☐ Rope
- ☐ Toilet paper and paper towels
- ☐ Moist towelettes
- ☐ Feminine supplies and personal hygiene items

... any other supplies as needed, from Appendix 1-3

APPENDIX 5
"EMERGENCY PET KIT" CHECKLIST

- ☐ Pet Safety App for lost pets: https://www.aspca.org/pet-care/general-pet-care/aspca-mobile-app
- ☐ Pet first aid kit
- ☐ Food
- ☐ Water
- ☐ Container bowls for food and water
- ☐ Towels
- ☐ Extra Collar
- ☐ Extra leash
- ☐ Medical records
- ☐ Two-week supply of medications
- ☐ Crate or sturdy carrier
- ☐ Blanket
- ☐ Recent photo of your pets in case of separation
- ☐ Toys and bones
- ☐ Disposable litter trays
- ☐ Disposable garbage bags
- ☐ Litter or P-Pads

PRAYER

Almighty Father, You are the name above all names, and we remember Yours is the prevailing name above (the name of this hurricane). We pray Your powerful protection over our families, pets and property and friends.

Give us Your peace that surpasses all understanding as we go through this storm.

Hold us close within the loving protection of Your hands.

In Jesus name, we pray, Amen.

BONUS DOWNLOAD:

Request your printable PDF of the five checklists that correspond to this book by emailing: megydavis@megydavis.com

The Disaster Survival Series

is a series of five books that are currently a work in progress. I see the following needs as urgent, so am simultaneously writing the next three non-fiction titles due out in 2019:

Wildfire Preparation and Survival

Winter Storm Preparation and Survival

Tornado Preparation and Survival

Due out in 2020:

Hail Storm Preparation and Survival

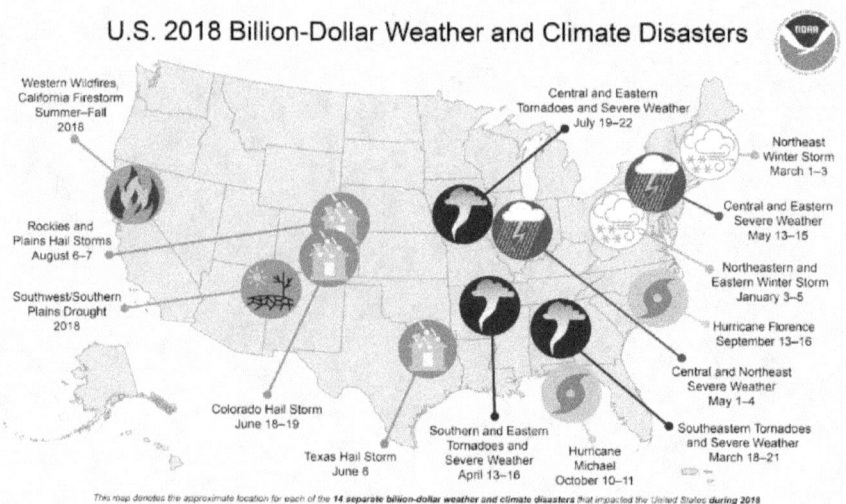

AUTHOR BIOGRAPHY

As a South Florida resident since 1972, I am a veteran of hurricane survival. My career as an author began in 2009, and I have published a novel every two and a half years since.

I plan to complete the five books of my **"Disaster Survival Series"** within the next nine months. I passionately believe that getting concise, geographic-specific vital information to the public for seasonal natural disasters can save homes, heartache and possibly lives.

We live in a mobile culture and a family moving from a winter storm-prone area to a hurricane-prone, tornado or wildfire-prone area needs specific and timely survival information.

I have been a professional photographer, a catastrophic insurance adjuster, and have traveled three continents teaching English as a second language. My photographic images are sold in my Etsy store, ***StockPhotoCo.*** With God as the wind in my sails, I have always considered life to be a too-short span of time, with creative opportunities to be embraced and pursued.

My dog Lexie proofreads, corrects punctuation and rephrases passive verbs for me.

www.ingramcontent.com/pod-product-compliance
Lightning Source LLC
Chambersburg PA
CBHW052116070526
44584CB00017B/2514